STEP-UP
HISTORY

Mary, Queen of Scots

Rhona Dick

Evans

Published by Evans Brothers Limited
2A Portman Mansions
Chiltern Street
London W1U 6NR

© Evans Brothers Limited 2007

Produced for Evans Brothers Limited by
White-Thomson Publishing Ltd,
Bridgewater Business Centre,
210 High Street,
Lewes, East Sussex BN7 2NH

Printed in Hong Kong by New Era Printing Co.Ltd.

Project manager: Ruth Nason

Designer: Carole Binding

Consultant: Dr Raymond McCluskey, Faculty of
Education, University of Glasgow

British Library Cataloguing in Publication Data

Dick, Rhona

Mary, Queen of Scots. - (Step-up history)
1. Mary, Queen of Scots, 1542-1587 - Juvenile
literature 2. Scotland - Kings and rulers -
Biography - Juvenile literature 3. Scotland -
History - Mary Stuart, 1542-1567 - Juvenile
literature

I. Title
941.1'05'092

ISBN-13: 9780237532048
ISBN-10: 0237532042

Picture acknowledgements:

The Bridgeman Art Library: pages 8 (Bibliotheque
Nationale, Paris, France/Lauros/Giraudon), 13t
(Burghley House Collection, Lincolnshire), 26
(Private Collection/© Richard Philp, London); Mary
Evans Picture Library: pages 5l, 6, 12, 13b, 15l, 16;
The National Archives: page 22; www.scran.ac.uk:
pages 14 and cover, top left (James Gardiner), 19
(Crown Copyright reproduced courtesy of Historic
Scotland), 20b and cover, top right (Lennoxlove
House Ltd), 23t (National Library of Scotland), 24
(Lennoxlove House Ltd), 27 (Trustees of the Blair
Museum); Topfoto.co.uk: pages 1, 9, 10 and cover,
11, 15r, 17t, 17b, 18, 20t, 23b, 25t, 25b.

Illustrative work by Carole Binding.

Contents

Who was Mary, Queen of Scots?

Mary was the daughter of James V of Scotland and his wife Mary of Guise. She was born on 8 December 1542 in Linlithgow Palace. Less than a week later James V died and, as his only surviving child, Mary became queen.

Scotland and England

For centuries English kings had tried to make Scotland part of the English kingdom. In 1314 the Scots defeated the English army at the Battle of Bannockburn, and a few years afterwards England accepted that Scotland was a separate kingdom. However, some skirmishes still took place and English monarchs did not really give up hope of enlarging their kingdom. This was true of Henry VIII, the king of England at the time of Mary's birth.

Henry VIII's eldest sister, Margaret, had married James IV of Scotland. Find her on the family tree below and work out how Mary, Queen of Scots was related to the Tudors.

▼ *The Tudor royal family is shown in red. Their symbol was a red and white rose. Henry VIII wanted Mary, Queen of Scots to marry his son Edward, because this would unite the Scottish and English thrones.*

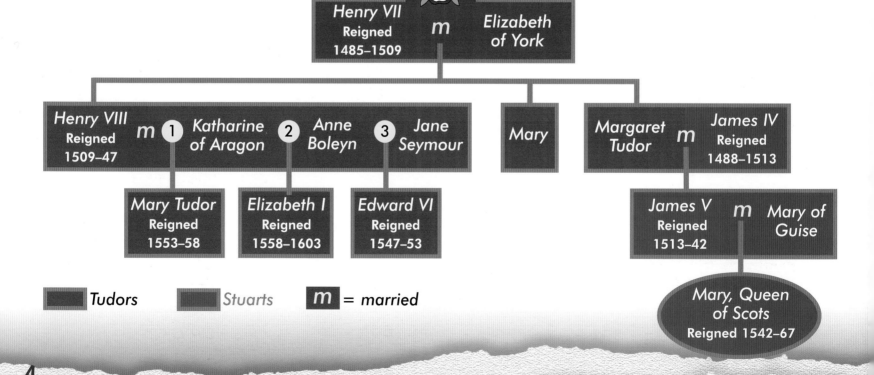

Henry VII
Reigned 1485–1509

m

Elizabeth of York

Henry VIII
Reigned 1509–47

m ① Katharine of Aragon ② Anne Boleyn ③ Jane Seymour

Mary

Margaret Tudor m James IV Reigned 1488–1513

Mary Tudor
Reigned 1553–58

Elizabeth I
Reigned 1558–1603

Edward VI
Reigned 1547–53

James V
Reigned 1513–42

m Mary of Guise

Mary, Queen of Scots
Reigned 1542–67

Tudors   Stuarts   m = married

▶ *This timeline shows the Scottish and English monarchs whose reigns began in the sixteenth century. Some were very young when they came to the throne and Regents ruled in their name.*

About this book

In this book you will find out about some of the people who influenced Mary's life and what happened as a result of their actions.

▲ James Stewart, Earl of Moray, was Mary's half brother. Sometimes he supported Mary, but at other times he fought against her.

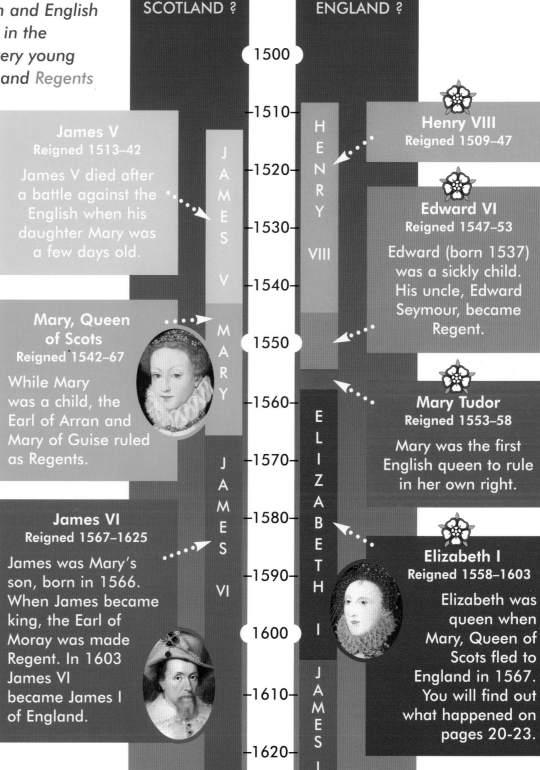

WHO RULED SCOTLAND ?

WHO RULED ENGLAND ?

1500

1510

James V
Reigned 1513–42

James V died after a battle against the English when his daughter Mary was a few days old.

J A M E S V

H E N R Y VIII

Henry VIII
Reigned 1509–47

1520

1530

Edward VI
Reigned 1547–53

Edward (born 1537) was a sickly child. His uncle, Edward Seymour, became Regent.

1540

Mary, Queen of Scots
Reigned 1542–67

While Mary was a child, the Earl of Arran and Mary of Guise ruled as Regents.

M A R Y

1550

1560

Mary Tudor
Reigned 1553–58

Mary was the first English queen to rule in her own right.

E L I Z A B E T H I

1570

James VI
Reigned 1567–1625

James was Mary's son, born in 1566. When James became king, the Earl of Moray was made Regent. In 1603 James VI became James I of England.

J A M E S VI

1580

Elizabeth I
Reigned 1558–1603

Elizabeth was queen when Mary, Queen of Scots fled to England in 1567. You will find out what happened on pages 20-23.

1590

1600

1610

J A M E S I

1620

1630

1640

5
••••

The life of a child queen

For safety Mary was taken to live at Stirling Castle, Inchmahome Priory and Dumbarton Castle (above), built on high rocky land jutting into the Clyde. Why would this be considered a safe place?

On 1 July 1543 Henry VIII and the Scottish Parliament signed a treaty agreeing to the marriage of Mary and Henry's son, Edward. The treaty stated that Mary would be brought up in England before her marriage, but many people in Scotland disliked this idea.

Henry VIII became impatient for Mary to move to England and for some years his armies raided the borders. This became known as 'The Rough Wooing'. Why is this a good name for these events?

On the move

Many Scottish noblemen feared that the English army could capture Mary, and so she was moved from place to place to try to keep her safe. Eventually it was decided to seek protection for her in France. Her mother, Mary of Guise, was a French noblewoman, and Scotland and France were old allies. With a small entourage Mary, Queen of Scots sailed to France from Dumbarton in August 1548.

Map labels:
0 — 50 miles
0 — 50 kilometres

• • • • = Mary's route to France

SCOTLAND
ATLANTIC OCEAN
Dumbarton
NORTH SEA
Edinburgh
Isle of Man
IRELAND
ENGLAND
WALES
ENGLISH CHANNEL
Roscoff
FRANCE

▲ Use the scale to find the length of Mary's journey to France. On this route English ships were less likely to intercept the small fleet.

A safe place to stay

Write a letter to Mary of Guise from one of the queen's guardians, explaining why you think Dumbarton Castle is a suitable place for Mary to stay before she sails for France. Give as many persuasive reasons as you can.

Life in France

Mary was brought up at the French court with the Dauphin and his brothers and sisters. When she arrived she spoke only Scots, but she quickly learned French. For the rest of her life she preferred to speak and write in French.

Mary was also taught to speak and read Latin, Italian, Spanish and some Greek. She learned to draw, dance, sing and play the lute. Two chaplains supervised her education in the Catholic faith. She was a good horsewoman and loved to go hunting.

Her clothes were made of the richest taffeta. She loved the balls and banquets in the luxurious French palaces, which were very different from bleak Scottish castles.

Mary becomes queen of France

On 24 April 1558, Mary and the Dauphin, François, were married in Paris. Just over a year later King Henri II of France died, and François and Mary became king and queen.

Their happiness didn't last long. Mary's mother died in Scotland in June 1560. In December François developed an ear infection which proved fatal. In 1561, aged 18, Mary, the dowager queen of France, returned to Scotland.

The Reformation

Mary lived during a period of great change called the Reformation, when people in several countries in Europe rejected many beliefs and practices of the Church. For example, they wanted to stop the system where people could buy forgiveness for their sins. Monasteries were amassing wealth and not keeping to the simple way of life that monks should follow.

Among others, Martin Luther in Germany and John Calvin from France said that the Church was becoming too worldly. They wanted it to be more spiritual and to have simpler ways of worship. People who followed these ideas about religious reform were called Protestants.

In many countries the Reformation was a bloody time. People refusing to follow the religion chosen by their ruler were executed in horrific ways. This picture shows what sometimes happened in England.

How the ideas spread

The new ideas spread partly because, after the printing press was invented in about 1450, Bibles and other literature could be printed in any language. It was no longer possible to suppress new ideas by burning manuscripts.

Before the Reformation all church services were conducted in Latin. Only well-educated people could understand the words. But Protestant preachers in the reformed churches spoke to the congregations in their own languages. Some people hated this idea so much that they rioted.

Scotland becomes Protestant

John Knox (1514?-72) was a Scottish priest who came to share Calvin's ideas. He left the priesthood, went to study in Europe and returned to Scotland in 1559.

Mary of Guise, who remained Queen Regent while Mary, Queen of Scots was in France, was opposed to religious reform. However, Knox was a persuasive preacher and by 1560 Parliament passed a law adopting Protestantism for Scotland. Mary of Guise never gave this law the assent that was needed from the monarch for all new laws.

From that time it was forbidden to say or hear Mass in Scotland, but the Catholic faith was not swept away. Many Scottish people continued to worship in Catholic ways, often in secret.

▶ *This statue of John Knox is at St Giles Cathedral, Edinburgh. He was minister there from 1560 until his death in 1572.*

Mary's faith

When Mary, Queen of Scots returned to Scotland in 1561, she held strongly to the Catholic faith. The Earl of Moray, her half brother, promised that Mass could be said in her private chapel at Holyrood Palace, even though he himself was a Protestant.

John Knox had several meetings with Mary and tried very hard to persuade her to become a Protestant. It is said that she feared Knox more than any man in her kingdom. In their discussions she made it clear that she would never give up her Catholic faith. She also said that she would not interfere in the religious beliefs of her subjects.

John Knox

Use published or ICT resources to help you write an obituary of John Knox. Remember to include his bad as well as his good points. You will need to use several sources to get a balance of opinions.

Mary's return to Scotland

Mary landed at Leith on 19 August 1561, almost exactly thirteen years after she had left Scotland for France. Many Scottish people were curious about her. They thought of her as a Catholic foreigner. Mary soon put them at their ease, greeting the welcoming party in Scots and assuring the people that she would not interfere with their choice of faith.

That night in Edinburgh a crowd of 500 people played musical instruments and sang outside Holyrood Palace. In the morning Mary thanked them, despite having had almost no sleep!

A stranger in a strange land

Mary must have felt strange on her return to Scotland. The castles where she stayed were little more than fortified towers, with none of the French luxuries, although Holyrood Palace was an exception. Much of it had been rebuilt in the Renaissance style and French stonemasons had worked on it.

The Scottish landscape was quite bleak and the weather colder, windier and wetter than Mary had been used to. And there was the new religion.

The search for a husband

It was expected that Mary would marry again. In the sixteenth century many people believed that women were not able to rule alone. Also, by marrying, Mary could make a strong alliance with another country.

► *The crosses that Mary is wearing and holding are a sign of the importance to her of her Catholic faith.*

There were many possible suitors, including foreign kings and princes, but choosing a husband was not easy. Mary hoped that Elizabeth I, who was now queen of England, would name Mary as her heir. Therefore Mary's choice of husband would need to be acceptable to Elizabeth. The choice of a Catholic husband would upset many Scottish people and be unacceptable to Elizabeth, who was Protestant. The choice of a Protestant husband would anger many European kingdoms. Poor Mary could not win!

In February 1564 Henry Stewart, Lord Darnley arrived from England. He was a cousin of Mary, and also had a claim on the English throne because he was related to the Tudors. Darnley was tall and good-looking. Like Mary, he enjoyed riding and hunting. He danced well and played the lute. They seemed well matched and Mary fell in love.

Pros and cons

One possible husband for Mary, Queen of Scots was Don Carlos, heir to the Spanish throne. Using the Internet or other published resources, find out about either Don Carlos or Lord Darnley. Then draw up a table of advantages and disadvantages of marriage to him.

▲ Mary was about 1.8m tall and Lord Darnley was one of the few men who was taller than her.

Margaret Tudor	m ①	James IV of Scotland	②	Archibald, 6th Earl of Angus

| James V | m | Mary of Guise | | Lady Mary Douglas | m | Matthew, Earl of Lennox |

| Mary, Queen of Scots | | Henry, Lord Darnley |

◀ Margaret Tudor was the grandmother of both Mary, Queen of Scots and Lord Darnley.

Contrasting lives in Mary's Scotland

Here are two people's accounts of their daily lives in the 1560s, when Mary was queen.

Jamie's life in the country

My family and I live in a wee house on the laird's land. We have simple food. Father sometimes traps hares and we can catch fish. Mother makes soup and bread. We are lucky to have a few chickens so we have fresh eggs, and we grow some vegetables. We have to work very hard, so there's not much time for play.

We're just off to sell some eggs at market in the local burgh. *It's not an easy journey because some of the roads are badly* rutted *and the bridges are dangerous. People who live near them are supposed to repair them, but they haven't time – it's hard enough to keep a family fed.*

The market town is very busy, with people selling all sorts of things: meat, fish, oatmeal, and eggs of course. Over there is a woman selling cloth. She must have a few sheep. I bet her daughters spin the wool before it's woven. You can use plants to dye the wool. The colours are dull browns and greens.

I can't read or write, but why would I need to? I can count and recognise coins. I've heard that the new church wants all boys to go to school, but who will do all the work then?

◀ Selling chickens at the market.

Jane's life at the palace

I'm one of her majesty's ladies. My life is comfortable at the palace. We have good food, plenty of meat and fine wine from France. On special occasions we have wonderful banquets and dancing.

▶ A sixteenth-century lady.

The queen wears the most beautiful gowns of fabrics dyed in rich colours, and she passes these on to us when she has finished with them. She has many wigs, too. Mary Seton, one of her ladies and close companions, styles the queen's hair beautifully.

There are lots of chambers here and they are decorated with heavy fabrics that keep the cold winds out. There are also paintings on the walls. The big fires keep us warm.

When she is at the palace, the queen meets important people and reads and writes many letters. She likes to listen to her secretary, David, singing and playing the lute.

We ladies are lucky that we can read and write, and speak French too. Most women in Scotland are not educated.

Chart the differences

Draw up a table like this to compare the lives of ordinary people and the royal household.

	Ordinary people	The Queen's household
Homes		
Food		
Clothing		
Education		
How I spend my time		

◀ Mary enjoyed fresh air and spent some of her time playing golf and croquet. This picture is not contemporary.

Mary and Darnley

Mary married Lord Darnley in July 1565, even though this choice of husband was not popular with all her noblemen, including her half brother, Moray. A Catholic wedding ceremony at Holyrood Abbey was followed by three days of celebrations. Darnley was given the title 'King of Scotland' and from then on, all official documents were signed by him as well as by Mary. The marriage was not happy and the king and queen spent more and more time apart

'Our most special servant'

David Riccio was an Italian secretary who was responsible for Mary's official letters. Darnley became jealous of him, especially because Mary called Riccio 'our most special servant'. Some of Mary's enemies persuaded Darnley to plot to murder Riccio. Perhaps they hoped that Mary would die too.

On 9 March 1566 Mary and some friends, including Riccio, were having supper in the small room adjoining the queen's bedchamber at Holyrood Palace. A group of men led by Darnley stormed up a narrow spiral staircase to the queen's apartments.

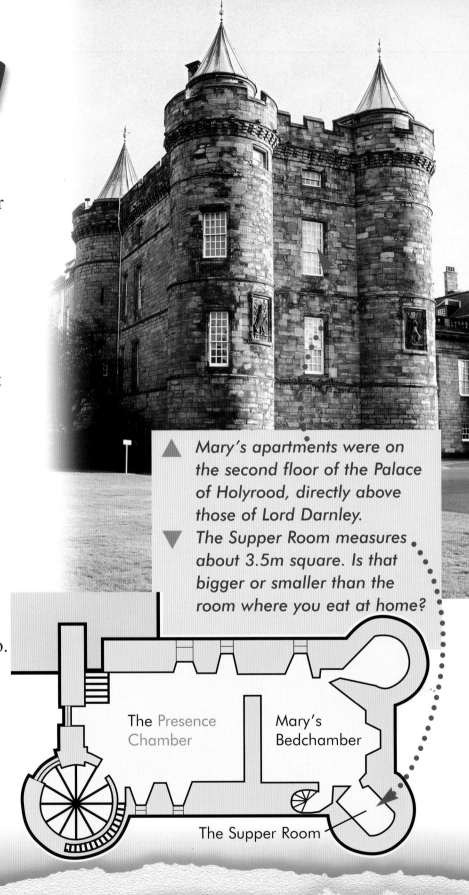

▲ Mary's apartments were on the second floor of the Palace of Holyrood, directly above those of Lord Darnley.
▼ The Supper Room measures about 3.5m square. Is that bigger or smaller than the room where you eat at home?

The Presence Chamber

Mary's Bedchamber

The Supper Room

One man pointed a gun at the queen, while others stabbed Riccio and dragged him to the Presence Chamber, where they left him to die. Mary was forcibly detained in the palace. The rebels' plan was to imprison her in Stirling Castle while Lord Darnley would rule Scotland.

Riccio was stabbed more than 50 times and Darnley's own dagger was left in his body.

Write a drama

Write a short drama about the murder of David Riccio. Act this out with your friends.

However, the day after Riccio's murder Mary persuaded Darnley to help her escape, by arguing that the rebels' plan would not give him any more power than he had with her as queen. She even promised to pardon the rebels. Mary and Darnley escaped from the palace and rode to Dunbar Castle. On 18 March Mary returned to Edinburgh at the head of an army of 8,000 men. The rebellion was defeated.

A new prince

Holyrood Palace was not safe enough for the queen and she moved to Edinburgh Castle. Here her son, Prince James, was born, on 19 June 1566.

£12,000 was raised from taxes to pay for his christening at Stirling Castle on 17 December. The king of France and Elizabeth I of England were two of the godparents, but they did not attend. Elizabeth sent a gold font, weighing about 12kg, as a gift. The ceremony was followed by fireworks and lavish masques. Lord Darnley, the child's father, was not there.

This is an artist's impression of Mary with her son James.

The death of Darnley

By the end of 1566 Mary regretted her marriage to Darnley. She hoped to find a way to be free of him, without endangering the right of their son, James, to become king after her death.

At this time Darnley was seriously ill in Glasgow. We don't know why, but on 20 January 1567 Mary went to Glasgow to bring him back to Edinburgh. Darnley then lodged with his servants in a house at Kirk o' Field and Mary spent much time there, nursing him, playing cards and dice, having supper and often spending the night. Darnley wrote to his father that he and Mary were happy together again.

On Sunday, 9 February, Mary was at Kirk o' Field again. In the evening she was reminded that she was due to attend a wedding masque and she returned to Holyrood. At about 2 am she was woken by the sound of an explosion. Later she learned that the house at Kirk o' Field had been destroyed and her husband was dead.

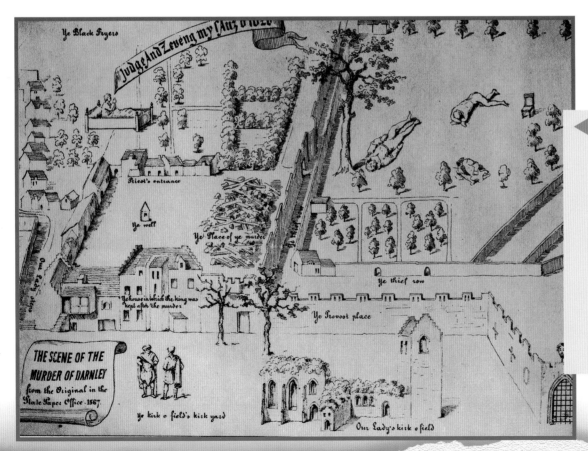

This engraving was made from a 1567 drawing. It shows the dead bodies of Darnley and his servant in the garden at Kirk o' Field, Edinburgh. In the top left corner the young Prince James is begging for justice. What else does the picture show?

The bodies of Darnley and his servant were found in the garden. They had been strangled. Mary seemed dazed and her doctors advised her to go to the country. It was reported that she played golf there, and people were shocked by this so soon after her husband's death.

Investigations and accusations

The person responsible for investigating the events was the Sheriff of Edinburgh, James Hepburn, Earl of Bothwell, but many people believed he was involved. Placards appeared in the streets, some naming Bothwell, some naming others as the murderer. One claimed that Mary knew of the assassination plot.

Darnley's father, the Earl of Lennox, accused Bothwell of the murder, and a private prosecution was heard by Parliament. Lennox was afraid to come to Edinburgh because it was full of Bothwell's men, and so the prosecution failed.

The Ainslie Bond

Shortly after the trial 27 nobles signed a bond in the Ainslie Tavern in Edinburgh. It marked their agreement to support Bothwell if Mary chose him as her new husband. Mary claimed that she refused his offer of marriage.

This placard suggested that Mary and Bothwell were involved in Darnley's death. M R stands for Maria Regina – Latin for Queen Mary. I H means James Hepburn. J was written as I in Latin. What do you think the ring of swords means?

James Hepburn, Earl of Bothwell.

Whodunnit

It is most often thought that Bothwell was responsible for Darnley's murder, but several other people also had motives. Write a detective story based on the murder of Darnley. Was Mary involved? Explain all the evidence at the end of your Whodunnit.

The end of a reign

Some of the common people turned against Mary because they believed she had been involved in Darnley's murder. The nobles were divided between those who were for the queen and those who wanted the crown to pass to her baby son, Prince James.

Mary's marriage to Bothwell

On Wednesday, 23 April 1567, Bothwell with 800 men intercepted Mary as she returned to Edinburgh from Stirling. They took her to Dunbar Castle. Some people think she was held against her will. Others think differently.

The queen was brought back to Edinburgh on 6 May and nine days later she and Bothwell were married in a Protestant service at Holyrood. There were no great celebrations, rich gifts or new clothes. People were shocked at the speed of events and called for Mary to leave Bothwell.

Many nobles who had once been loyal to Mary and Bothwell turned against them, including some of those who had signed the Ainslie Bond. They decided to depose Mary and make Prince James king.

▲ At Carberry Hill, Mary's half brother, the Earl of Moray, was with the army that opposed Mary. Moray's men held a banner showing Darnley dead and Prince James saying 'Judge and avenge my cause, O Lord'.

Surrender at Carberry Hill

Mary and her opponents both raised armies and on 15 June 1567 the two armies faced each other at Carberry Hill outside Edinburgh. There was no bloodshed and Mary negotiated a safe conduct for Bothwell while she surrendered.

The queen was taken to Lochleven Castle and held prisoner for over ten months. While she was there she was forced to abdicate in favour of her son, who became James VI. The Earl of Moray was named as Regent.

Lochleven Castle was an ideal prison as it was built on an island, making escape very difficult.

Mary flees Scotland

Mary would not accept that she had lost her throne. She tried to escape from Lochleven dressed as a washerwoman, but was recognised by the boatman and returned to the castle. On 2 May 1568 she did escape and rode towards Dumbarton Castle with an army of supporters.

On 13 May an army led by Moray defeated Mary's men at the village of Langside, near Glasgow. Mary's way to Dumbarton Castle was blocked and so she rode south with a few loyal followers to the Solway Firth. Here the decision had to be made whether to sail for France or to seek refuge in England.

Having reached the Solway Firth, Mary left Scotland for the last time on 16 May 1568.

Make a timeline

Draw a timeline to show the major events in Mary's life from her marriage to Darnley until she fled Scotland.

19

At Elizabeth's mercy

Mary could not be persuaded to flee to France. She believed that Queen Elizabeth of England would help her to get her throne back, and so she sailed across the Solway to England.

Shortly after she landed, a force of about 400 horsemen accompanied Mary to Carlisle Castle. She was guarded carefully for it was known that many Catholics believed Mary, not Elizabeth, should be queen of England. The windows of Mary's room were barred and soldiers kept guard outside the room at night. Although not officially a prisoner, Mary was accompanied by 100 men whenever she rode or walked outside the castle.

The Casket Letters

Elizabeth refused to meet Mary until it was proved that Mary had not been involved in the murder of Darnley. A conference was held to investigate. The Earl of Moray, who did not want Mary to return to Scotland, claimed to have found a silver casket containing letters that Mary had written to Bothwell. He said the letters proved her guilt.

▲ Elizabeth I was Protestant. Her advisers believed that Mary posed a threat.

▲ The letters that Moray claimed to have found in this casket were returned to him and have since disappeared. They were not signed or addressed to anyone. Do you think they could have been forged by someone in the queen's household?

Mary was not allowed to see the letters or the copies that were made of them. Eventually the commissioners said that there was not enough proof of Mary's guilt, but still she was kept under guard and not allowed to meet Elizabeth.

A more suitable residence

Carlisle was very close to the Scottish border and Elizabeth's advisers thought that some Scots, still loyal to Mary, might try to rescue her. Therefore Mary was moved to a castle in Yorkshire. While she was there she learned to write English.

For almost 19 years Mary was moved from one lodging to another in England, either so that the buildings could be thoroughly cleaned or for security. The residence she hated most was Tutbury Castle in Staffordshire. It was draughty, damp and her rooms were directly above the 'stinking midden'.

Passing the time

Mary had several 'gaolers' during her stay in England, some kinder than others. For many years the Earl of Shrewsbury and his wife, Bess of Hardwick, were responsible for her. Mary was allowed to keep dogs and caged birds and had a staff of about 40. She could also ride, hunt and practise archery. Bess and Mary spent many hours together sewing.

Questions and answers

For a long time historians have asked questions about the Casket Letters. No one knows the real answers. Use what you know about the people in this story to give possible answers to these questions:

- What could have happened to the original letters?

- Why was Mary not even allowed to see the copies that were made of them?

Now try to think of two more simple questions to ask about the letters.

Mary loved puzzles and codes. In one embroidery she included this design. The cat is said to represent Elizabeth and the mouse is Mary.

Plot and counterplot

While Mary was in England, there were many plots to free her or to make her queen of England. As the plots were discovered, her freedom was restricted.

Sir Francis Walsingham, a member of Queen Elizabeth's government, had spies all over Europe and was determined to find a way to have Mary executed. He recruited spies who pretended to support Mary. One devised a way of getting messages to and from her, hidden in beer barrels. Although Mary used codes, Walsingham knew what her messages said before they were delivered!

The Babington Plot

Sir Anthony Babington planned to organise an invasion from abroad, to free Mary and murder Elizabeth. In July 1586 he wrote to Mary explaining his plans, and ten days later she replied, approving them. Babington was arrested on 14 August. He confessed under torture and was executed.

Write in code

Mary often used codes in her letters, and devised symbols for common words.

Write a list of ten common words and devise symbols for those. Now invent a code for the alphabet. Write a short letter to a friend using your code.

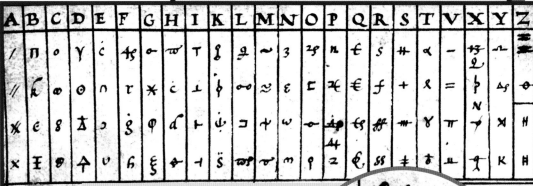

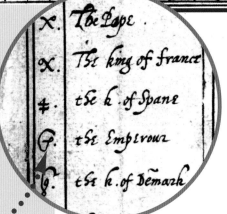

Here are four codes that Mary used. Why was it safer for her to use different codes when writing to different people? She also used symbols instead of people's names.

Sentenced to death

Mary was arrested and taken to Fotheringhay Castle, where she was tried for treason, found guilty and sentenced to death. When news of the death sentence spread abroad, the French ambassador protested, but in Scotland Mary's son, James VI, said nothing. He hoped to succeed Elizabeth and perhaps he thought that protesting would ruin his chances.

Elizabeth signed Mary's death warrant on 1 February 1587. After dinner on 7 February Mary was told that she would be executed the next morning. She spent her last night writing letters, making a will to share out her belongings, and in prayer. In the morning she went to the great hall where the block was placed. Two of her ladies were allowed to stay with her, provided that they made no noise.

Mary, Queen of Scots died true to her Catholic faith. Afterwards, to the shock of those present, Mary's little pet dog crawled out from under her skirts.

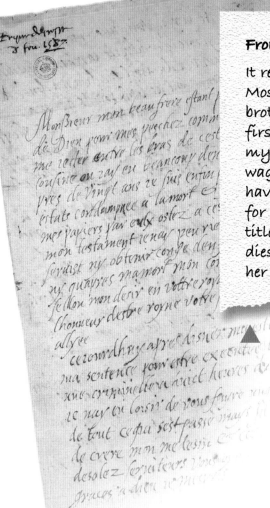

From Mary's last letter

It remains for me to beg Your Most Christian Majesty, my brother-in-law and old ally ... firstly by charity, in paying my unfortunate servants the wages due them ... further, by having prayers offered to God for a queen who has borne the title Most Christian, and who dies a Catholic, stripped of all her possessions.

▲ Mary wrote to her brother-in-law, the king of France, a few hours before her execution. She told him that she wanted to be buried in France. What two things does she ask him to do in this part of the letter?

▶ This picture of the execution was painted in 1608.

'In my end is my beginning'

After Mary's death everything involved in her execution was burned. Mary's heart was buried in the grounds of Fotheringhay Castle and her body was encased in a huge lead coffin. Sir Francis Walsingham wanted Mary to be buried in a local church without ceremony. However, at the end of July 1587 the coffin was taken in the middle of the night to Peterborough Cathedral, where it was buried with dignity the next day. An effigy taken from Mary's death mask was erected over her tomb.

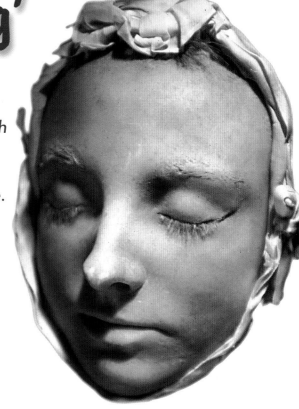

▶ A wax death mask was made of Mary's face.

Reactions to Mary's death

On hearing that Mary had been executed, Queen Elizabeth wept and went into mourning. She ordered the arrest of her secretary, Davison, who had passed her Mary's death warrant to sign. Davison was imprisoned and fined £10,000!

The Scottish people were very angry and some wanted to fight the English. James VI showed his grief in public.

In France a great memorial service was held for Mary in Notre Dame de Paris. This was the cathedral where Mary had been married in 1558 and also crowned queen of France.

At one time Mary had named Philip II, king of Spain, as her heir. He believed that he should now be king of England and in 1588 he launched a mighty fleet, the Spanish Armada, to invade England.

Explain the reactions

Why did Elizabeth I, James VI and Philip II behave the way they did after Mary's execution? List as many reasons as you can.

The union of the crowns

In 1603 Queen Elizabeth died and Mary's son, James VI, became James I of England. The crowns of Scotland and England were united. All British monarchs since that time are descended from Mary, Queen of Scots.

A new memorial

James ordered that a memorial for his mother should be built at Westminster Abbey in London. The magnificent white marble memorial took many years to finish, but in 1612 Mary's coffin was moved from Peterborough Cathedral and reburied in Westminster Abbey.

Fotheringhay Castle is now nothing more than a pile of rubble overgrown with grass. Most of the stones have been removed for use elsewhere and there is no memorial to the events that took place there.

Mary's motto

Mary's motto was 'In my end is my beginning'. Try to think why this is particularly appropriate.

The memorial at Westminster Abbey. Mary's effigy here was probably a copy of the one at Peterborough Cathedral.

How do we know what Mary was like?

People can find out about the past from several sources, including:

- contemporary documents such as letters, diaries, account books and inventories
- pictures
- artefacts.

This portrait of Mary was probably painted when she lived in France. What does it tell you about her appearance?

Eyewitness accounts

Some contemporary documents, such as letters and diaries, give eyewitness accounts of people and events. Sir Amyas Paulet, one of Mary's gaolers, kept a diary. In it he recorded that on Maundy Thursday 1585, despite being in prison and having very little money, Mary gave 42 girls and 18 boys more than one metre of woollen cloth each.

Robert Wynkfielde was an eyewitness at Mary's execution. His account tells us that Mary said this to her executioner:

> I forgive you with all my heart for now, I hope, you shall make an end of all my troubles.

Here are two more examples of information given by eyewitnesses:

> Mary, Queen of Scots hardly left her husband's bedside during his final illness. (Throckmorton, the English Ambassador)

> During meetings with notable people Mary often sat embroidering. (Thomas Randolph)

Wills and inventories

Mary wrote a will before the birth of her son. In this will she made 36 bequests to Darnley, even though she was separated from him.

The Inventories of the Queen of Scots record that Mary paid £125 for a wedding dress for Margaret Carwood, one of her ladies of the bedchamber. What could this infomation from the will and the Inventories tell you about Mary's character?

Artefacts

Mary had to leave many belongings behind when she fled to England, and others were sold or seized during her imprisonment. In her final will, written on the eve of her execution, Mary left her remaining possessions to her loyal servants.

Myths have grown up about artefacts said to have belonged to Mary, but few objects can definitely be traced back to her. We do know that many of the embroideries she worked on survive.

Primary and secondary sources

Primary sources are created at the time of the event. Secondary sources are created later – sometimes long after the events they describe or represent. Many pictures of Mary fall into this category. Do you think that secondary sources always provide reliable evidence about people and events? Give your reasons.

▶ *Few pictures of Mary were painted in her lifetime. Elizabeth Curle, one of Mary's ladies, paid for this portrait after Mary's execution. Why do you think she did that?*

Describe Mary

Use all the information you have found in this book to write two lists of adjectives that describe (1) Mary's appearance and (2) her character: for example, 'fashion conscious' and 'animal lover'. Beside each adjective write the source of your information.

Glossary

abdicate	to resign as queen or king.
alliance	a union between people or countries which will benefit both in some way.
allies	people or countries who have agreed to help one another.
artefacts	man-made objects. For example, metalwork or needlework.
assassination	a murder, usually of a famous or important person.
assent	agreement or consent.
bequests	gifts left by someone who has died, or promised in their will.
block	a large piece of wood. People who were to be beheaded knelt down and rested their neck on the block.
bond	a document that people sign showing that they all agree to something.
burgh	a town.
Catholic	a Christian who maintained the beliefs and many of the traditions of the medieval Church and continued to recognise the authority of the Pope after the Reformation.
chamber	a room.
chaplain	a priest who ministers to members of a family.
commissioners	representatives of Mary and the Earl of Moray, who acted as judges.
conference	a meeting to discuss important matters.
congregation	a group of people attending a church.
contemporary	from, or made at, the time.
Dauphin	the title of the eldest son of the French king. Pronounced 'dough-fan'.
death mask	a wax or plaster cast taken of a face after death.
depose	to overthrow.
dowager queen	a king's widow, who cannot reign.
effigy	a likeness of a person in metal or stone, often used on tombs.
entourage	a group of attendants. Mary's entourage included her guardian, her governess, two half brothers and four attendants, all called Mary.
fatal	causing death.
font	a stone or metal vessel to hold the water used at baptisms.
fortified	strengthened to withstand attacks.
half brother	Mary and the Earl of Moray had the same father but different mothers, so he was her half brother.
heir	a person who will inherit goods or a title when the present holder dies.
intercept	to stop and seize on the way from one place to another.
inventories	lists of possessions often made when people died. Inventories of Mary's possessions were made regularly.
manuscripts	handwritten documents.
masque	a masked ball or costume drama.
Mass	a service in the Catholic Church.

Maundy Thursday	the day before Good Friday when monarchs traditionally give gifts to poor people, one for each year of the monarch's life.
midden	a rubbish heap.
monarch	a king or queen who rules a country.
monasteries	religious buildings where monks live and work.
motto	a phrase, sometimes in Latin, often used by a family on their coat of arms.
mourning	grieving for someone who has died.
negotiate	to discuss, in order to reach an agreement.
obituary	a short news article about the life story of someone who has died.
Parliament	a meeting of important people from all over the country, to pass laws and provide money for the monarch.
placard	a poster.
Presence Chamber	a room next to the queen's private chambers, for formal meetings.
prosecution	a court case in which someone is accused of something.
Protestant	a Christian who rejected many aspects of the medieval Church in favour of the ideas of the Reformation.
raid	to make a sudden attack.
Reformation	a period in the sixteenth century when new ideas about religious practices and beliefs spread across Europe.
Regent	a person who rules for a monarch who is a child or is living in another country.
Renaissance	an age of change in architecture, arts and literature.
rutted	furrowed, uneven or potholed.
safe conduct	a pass that allowed someone to travel without being arrested.
skirmishes	minor fights, smaller than battles.
source	a place where you find information.
spiritual	holy, pious or not concerned with worldly matters.
Stuarts	the royal family of Scotland from 1371 to 1603, and of Scotland and England from 1603 to 1714. Mary changed the spelling of the name Stewart to Stuart.
succeed	to inherit the throne when the present monarch dies.
suitors	men who pay attention to someone because they hope to marry her.
suppress	to cover up or stamp out, in order to stop from spreading.
surviving child	a child who lives after their brothers and sisters have died.
taffeta	an expensive silk fabric.
treason	betraying a monarch or a country.
treaty	a written agreement.
Tudors	England's royal family, 1485-1603.
will	a document that explains what you want to be done with your possessions when you die.
wooing	trying to gain the affection of someone, particularly a person you want to marry.

For teachers and parents

This book is designed to develop children's knowledge, understanding and skills in Environmental Studies with a Scottish focus within the Renaissance and Reformation period. Reference is made to contemporary events in France and England as they impacted upon the life of Mary, Queen of Scots and her subjects.

Throughout the book and in the associated activities children are encouraged to consider the chronology of events and the nature of the available historical evidence. Whilst providing guidance, the activities are designed to act as a starting point for children's further research, and in every case the children should plan their work carefully, select from the information available and present their findings appropriately.

The activities are designed principally to develop history skills but often make links with other curriculum subjects, and children are encouraged to use ICT where appropriate, particularly for further research and presentation. The book also gives opportunities for developing responsible attitudes to others.

Mary, Queen of Scots is an enigmatic and romantic character, and facts have become entwined with myth. Much of our information about her comes from contemporary documents including Mary's own letters, but there are other sources. Mary related an account of the major events of her life to her secretary, but even this must be viewed with caution as human memory is not infallible and often biased. Some of the pictures of Mary were painted centuries after her death, and are therefore just an artist's interpretation. Children must be encouraged to recognise the possible pitfalls here and to evaluate the evidence with care.

SUGGESTED FURTHER ACTIVITIES

Pages 4 – 5 Who was Mary, Queen of Scots?
As so many Scottish monarchs had been minors, the power of the nobles had grown. When James V died, leaving a baby as queen, the nobles saw further opportunities to increase their power. The clan system also meant that, for many, their first loyalty was to family, not to crown.

Children could find out more about Mary of Guise, who remained as dowager queen in Scotland when her daughter was in France. They could consider why she thought it more important to govern in Scotland than to accompany her daughter to France.

Pages 6 – 7 The life of a child queen
The children could write a document from an adviser of either Henry VIII of England or Henri II of France, explaining why it would be good for Scotland if Mary were to be married to his son.

Children could research aspects of entertainments, for example dance and jousting. (Henri II of France died in a joust.)

They could use a portrait of the Dauphin to write a description of him.

Pages 8 – 9 The Reformation
Children could research the lives of Martin Luther, John Calvin and Ignatius of Loyola, and create a timeline that identifies the major events of the Reformation in different countries in Europe.

Children could compare the details of the deaths of George Wishart and Cardinal Beaton and consider in what ways they might be linked.

Children could find out about Henry VIII's attitude to the Church in England between 1521 and 1538. Did the Reformation in England follow the same pattern as the rest of Europe?

Pages 10 – 11 Mary's return to Scotland
Mary was ill-prepared, in political terms, for life in Scotland. She was only 18 and, although intelligent and articulate, had little experience of what monarchy meant in her homeland – particularly the ambitious and often self-seeking scheming of the nobles, including her half brother, the Earl of Moray, whom she trusted.

The children could make simple comparisons between Mary's life in France and her life in Scotland: for example, her homes, the language she spoke, and how she passed her time.

A biography of Don Carlos is at http://www.xs4all.nl/~kvenjb/madmonarchs/doncarlos/doncarlos_bio.htm.

Pages 12 – 13 Contrasting lives in Mary's Scotland
To find out more about the everyday life of ordinary people living in Scotland at this time, children could investigate http://www.bbc.co.uk/scotland/education/as/burghlife/. This is an interactive site about the lives of people who lived and worked near Stirling in 1566.

Pages 14 – 15 Mary and Darnley
In the hall or playground, or on large sheets of paper, children could mark out the size of the Supper Room in Mary's apartments, and add the fireplace and furniture that would have been in the room. Bearing in mind the clothing people wore, they should comment on what it must have been like when the armed men burst in to seize Riccio.

Children could read the words said on behalf of Elizabeth when she sent the christening gift and comment on their tone. Go to http://www.geo.ed.ac.uk/scotgaz/towns/townhistory538.html and search for 'font'. The children could then write an appropriate reply.

Pages 16 – 17 The death of Darnley

Children could write a newspaper article about the death of Darnley, hinting at who might be responsible.

Children could read transcripts of statements made by some of the witnesses from Kirk o' Field and list the questions they would have asked the witnesses. The National Archives have transcripts of the witness statements as well as tasks associated with the plan of the assassination: http://www.learningcurve.gov.uk/snapshots/snapshot02/snapshot2.htm.

Pages 18 – 19 The end of a reign

Mary enjoyed dressing up. As a child in France she sometimes dressed in ordinary Scottish clothing. She was known to leave Holyrood and ride around Edinburgh in disguise. When Mary escaped from Borthwick Castle, before the events of Carberry Hill, she was dressed as a man. To try to escape from Lochleven she dressed as a washerwoman. The children could compare and contrast the two events and write down as many things as they can that might have given away Mary's identity as she tried to escape from Lochleven Castle.

When Mary fled from the Battle of Langside and reached the Solway Firth, some of her companions urged her to sail to France instead of seeking refuge in England. Children could write a speech in which they try to persuade Mary that it would be safer to go to France.

Pages 20 – 21 At Elizabeth's mercy

Children could draw a picture as a design for an embroidery, which embodies a device representing part of Mary's life. The most famous one is of the cat and the mouse, but how might Mary represent her half brother, the Earl of Moray, or one of her husbands?

Mary often devised anagrams of her name (Mary Stuart) with V standing for U in Stuart. This is another example of Mary's love of puzzles. Children could make anagrams of the names of important people in Mary's life.

Children could investigate the relationship between Mary and Elizabeth through transcripts of their correspondence. They could think about the problems that Mary's arrival in England created for Elizabeth.

Mary said that people in her household knew her writing well enough to be able to have forged the Casket Letters. Which major characters in Mary's life might have wanted the letters forged and why?

Pages 22 – 23 Plot and counterplot

Plot the locations of Mary's incarceration on a map of England: Carlisle Castle, Bolton Castle in Yorkshire, Chatsworth House in Derbyshire, Coventry Castle, Tutbury Castle, Sheffield Manor, Wingfield Manor near Matlock, Tixall Hall near Stafford, Chartley Park near Stafford, Fotheringhay Castle near Peterborough. Let the children suggest why these were in the Midlands, not near the Scottish border or closer to London.

Read a contemporary description of Mary's execution from one of the following websites: http://englishhistory.net/tudor/exmary.html or http://tudorhistory.org/primary/exmary.html. Eyewitness accounts are also at http://www.eyewitnesstohistory.com/maryqueenofscots.htm. Then ask the children to draw the event. Compare the drawings and comment on differences. This will help children to understand that history can be interpreted differently.

The watercolour of the execution scene on page 23 was painted in 1608. It shows the Earls of Kent and Shrewsbury seated to the right, the Dean of Peterborough exhorting Mary to repent, and her physician, steward and two men servants kneeling. Her favourite women attendants, Jane Kennedy and Elizabeth Curle, stand weeping. Children could consider where the artist obtained his information.

Elizabeth secretly hoped that Mary would be murdered before the death sentence could be carried out. Children could consider why.

Pages 24 – 25 'In my end is my beginning'

Children could create an interactive timeline with hyperlinks to text and images about the major events in Mary's life. Alternatively they could use a map as the home page of their multimedia presentation. They could also add links to people who influenced what happened.

Pages 26 – 27 How do we know what Mary was like?

Playing Chinese whispers is one way of demonstrating how facts can become distorted through time.

Ask the children to locate as many portraits of Mary as they can and to identify which are contemporary and which are later interpretations.

Children could write an entry for Mary for a historical 'Who's Who?', describing events in her life and giving reasons for her actions.

BOOKS AND WEBSITES

There are many general biographies of Mary, and some that focus on aspects of her reign, such as the Casket Letters or the Babington Plot.

John Guy, *My Heart is My Own: The life of Mary, Queen of Scots* (Fourth Estate/HarperPerennial, 2004)
Antonia Fraser, *Mary, Queen of Scots* (Weidenfeld and Nicholson, 2002)
Elizabeth Eisenberg, *The Captive Queen in Derbyshire* (Wye Valley Press, 1984)

Not all of the numerous websites about Mary are accurate. Children should be encouraged to question their reliability. Recommended are:
http://englishhistory.net/tudor/relative/maryqosbio.html
http://www.aboutscotland.com/mqshfra.html
http://www.marie-stuart.co.uk/France/France.htm

High-quality pictorial resources and original documents can be found at http://www.scran.ac.uk/, an online learning resource service with free access for Scottish schools.

Index